Pebble® Plus

Life around the World
Shopping in Many Cultures

by Martha E. H. Rustad

Consulting Editor: Gail Saunders-Smith, PhD

Capstone press

Mankato, Minnesota

Pebble Plus is published by Capstone Press,
151 Good Counsel Drive, P.O. Box 669, Mankato, Minnesota 56002.
www.capstonepress.com

1 2 3 4 5 6 13 12 11 10 09 08

Library of Congress Cataloging-in-Publication Data
Rustad, Martha E. H. (Martha Elizabeth Hillman), 1975–
    Shopping in many cultures/by Martha E. H. Rustad.
    p. cm. — (Pebble plus. Life around the world)
    Summary: "Simple text and photographs present shopping in many cultures" — Provided by publisher.
    Includes bibliographical references and index.
    ISBN-13: 978-1-4296-1743-7 (hardcover)
    ISBN-10: 1-4296-1743-8 (hardcover)
    1. Shopping — Cross-cultural studies — Juvenile literature. I. Title. II. Series.
TX335.5.R87 2009
306.3 — dc22   2008003583

Editorial Credits

Sarah L. Schuette, editor; Kim Brown, book designer; Alison Thiele, set designer; Wanda Winch, photo researcher

Photo Credits

AP Images/Aaron Favila, 13
Art Life Images/Inger Helene Boasson, 7
Capstone Press/Karon Dubke, 1, 15
The Image Works/Jeff Greenberg, 9; Richard Lord, 17; Visum Silke Reents, 21
Landov LLC/Xinhua, 19
Peter Arnold/Jean-Leo Dugast, cover
Shutterstock/David Kay, 11; Pavel Losevsky, 5

Note to Parents and Teachers

The Life around the World set supports national social studies standards related to
culture and geography. This book describes and illustrates shopping in many cultures.
The images support early readers in understanding the text. The repetition of words and
phrases helps early readers learn new words. This book also introduces early readers
to subject-specific vocabulary words, which are defined in the Glossary section. Early
readers may need assistance to read some words and to use the Table of Contents,
Glossary, Read More, Internet Sites, and Index sections of the book.

Table of Contents

Shopping

People shop in every culture.

They buy food, clothing,

and other items they need.

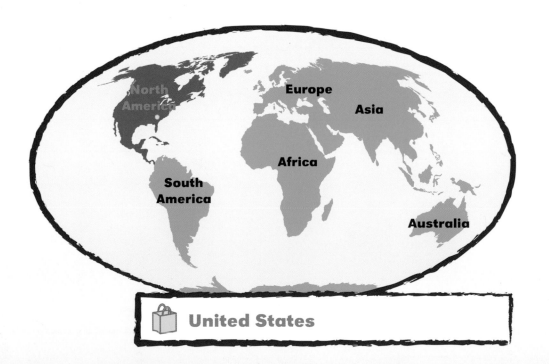

United States

Shopping for Food

Shoppers in Norway
buy fish at
an outdoor market.

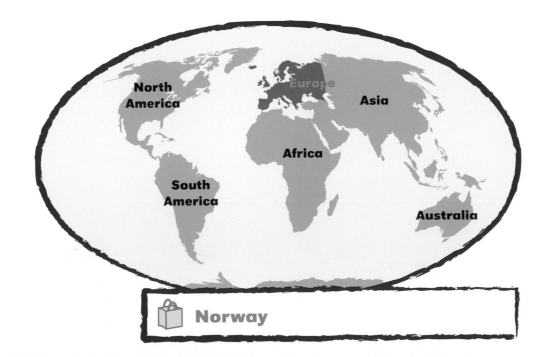

Norway

7

A girl in Canada
orders lunch at a deli.

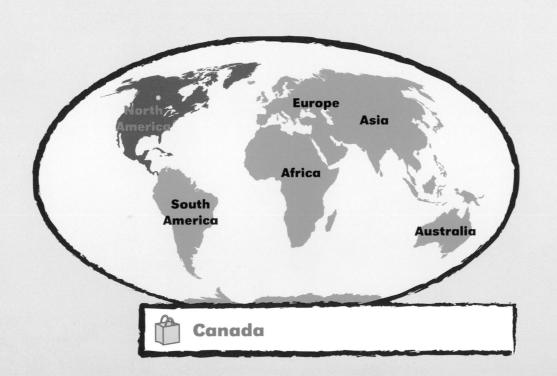

Canada

A woman in Morocco
shops for spices.

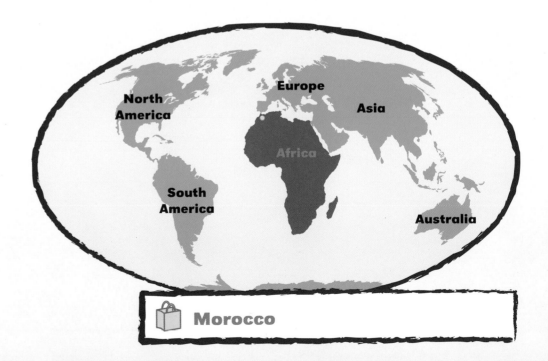

Morocco

Shoppers in the Philippines
buy grapes and oranges.

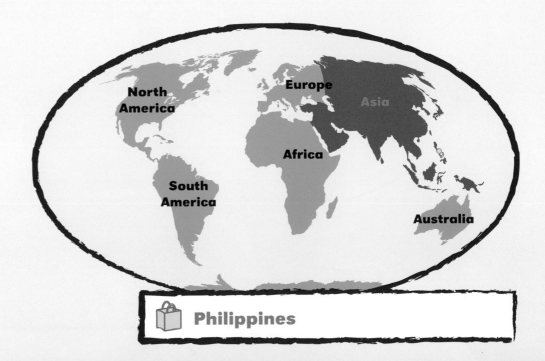

Philippines

Other Items

A girl in the United States shops for new clothes.

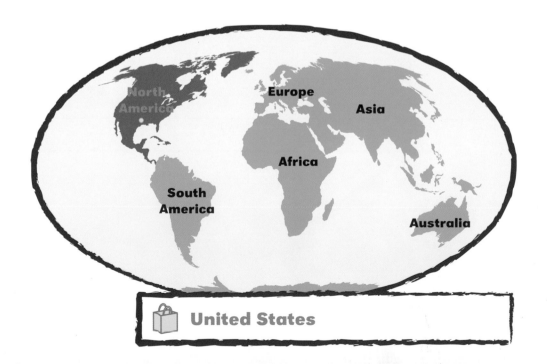

United States

A mother in Guatemala

buys clothespins

at a department store.

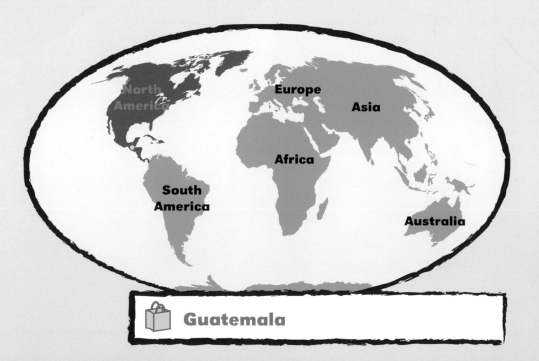

Guatemala

A family in China
looks for a red lantern
at a market.

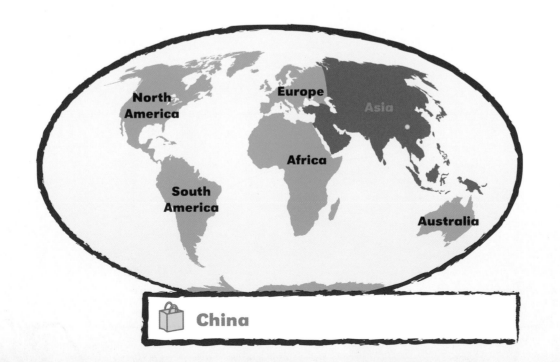

North
America

Europe

Asia

Africa

South
America

Australia

China

At Home

Around the world,
people shop at
many different places.
Where do you shop?

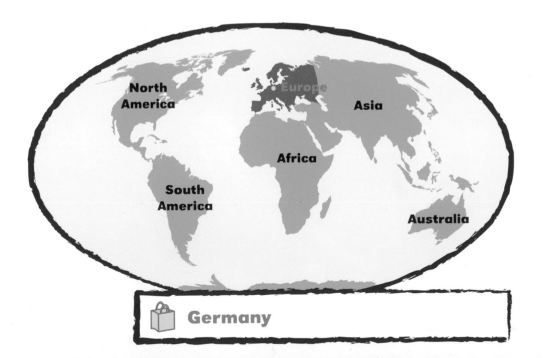

North America

Europe

Asia

Africa

South America

Australia

Germany

Glossary

culture — the way of life, ideas, customs, and traditions of a group of people

deli — a store that sells different kinds of food already prepared

department store — a large store that sells clothing, household items, appliances, and other things people need

lantern — a light with a frame around it; lanterns have paper, glass, or metal frames.

market — a place where people buy and sell food or goods

spice — a substance used to flavor foods

Read More

Gillis, Jennifer Blizin. *Neighborhood Shopping.* My Neighborhood. Vero Beach, Fla.: Rourke, 2007.

Hill, Mary. *Signs at the Store.* Signs in My World. New York: Children's Press, 2003.

Roy, Jennifer Rozines, and Gregory Roy. *Money at the Store.* Math All Around. New York: Marshall Cavendish Benchmark, 2007.

Internet Sites

FactHound offers a safe, fun way to find Internet sites related to this book. All of the sites on FactHound have been researched by our staff.

Here's how:

1. Visit *www.facthound.com*

2. Choose your grade level.

3. Type in this book ID **1429617438** for age-appropriate sites. You may also browse subjects by clicking on letters, or by clicking on pictures and words.

4. Click on the **Fetch It** button.

FactHound will fetch the best sites for you!

Index

Word Count: 92
Grade: 1
Early-Intervention Level: 18